Breaking The Chains Of Leukemia

The Blinatumomab Era in Acute Lymphoblastic Leukemia (ALL)

By

Dr. Alice E. Rendon

Disclaimer

The information provided in this book is intended for general informational purposes only. It is not a substitute for professional medical advice, diagnosis, or treatment. Readers should not rely on the information in this book for making medical decisions or determining appropriate courses of action. Always seek the advice of your physician or other qualified healthcare provider with any questions you may have regarding a medical condition. The author and publisher of this book are not responsible for any specific health or medical outcomes resulting from the use of information presented herein. The content is based on knowledge available up to the book's publication date, and subsequent developments in medical science may impact the accuracy of the information provided. The inclusion of specific treatments, drugs, or therapies does not imply endorsement or recommendation. Readers are encouraged to consult relevant medical professionals for personalized advice tailored to their individual health needs.

Table Of Contents

Introduction

One of the most dangerous diseases in the field of hematological cancers is acute lymphoblastic leukemia (ALL), which is defined by the unchecked growth of immature lymphoid cells. This is an aggressive blood cancer that affects both adults and children, primarily focusing on lymphoid precursors. One must explore the complex terrain of ALL in order to fully appreciate the significance of recent discoveries, especially the function of blinatumomab.

When lymphoid progenitor cells develop abnormally, malignant blasts build up in the bone marrow and peripheral blood, which is the cause of ALL. At around 25% of all childhood cancer diagnoses, it is the most prevalent type of the disease. Though less frequently, adults can also become victims of this unrelenting illness.

Numerous symptoms, many of which are nonspecific, such as fatigue, fever, unexplained weight loss, bone pain, and recurrent infections, are indicative of the disease. ALL progresses quickly, making early diagnosis and treatment essential.

Chemotherapy has traditionally been the mainstay of ALL treatment, with the goal of eliminating the leukemic cells and bringing about remission. Even though many patients respond well to chemotherapy in the beginning, there is always a chance that they will relapse, which makes novel therapeutic approaches necessary.

Thanks to developments in supportive care and treatment protocols, children with ALL have experienced significant improvements in their outcomes over the years. For some patients, especially adults and those with high-risk characteristics, the path to remission and long-term survival is still difficult.

The search for safer and more effective treatments has been a defining feature of ALL research. The investigation of immunotherapies and targeted therapies has accelerated, presenting a paradigm change in the field of medicine. Of these, blinatumomab stands out as a promising treatment option for patients with ALL.

Bispecific T-cell engagers, or BiTEs, like blinatumomab, are a new class of immunotherapeutic drugs that aim to use the immune system to fight cancer. By binding to both cancer and T cells at the same time, its mechanism of action increases the cytotoxicity of T cells, which aids in the destruction of malignant cells. This novel strategy has the potential to overcome the drawbacks of conventional chemotherapy and the difficulties associated with minimal residual disease (MRD) in ALL patients.

It is critical to comprehend the background and current status of ALL treatments as we navigate the complexities of ALL and the changing landscape of cancer therapeutics. The context of patients', doctors', and researchers' struggles provides the groundwork for investigating how blinatumomab might change the way that people think about ALL treatments. The insights from recent clinical trials will be unpacked in the sections that follow, providing light on how blinatumomab might redefine the norm for treating ALL patients who are in remission.

Significance Of Minimal Residual Disease (MRD)

The concept of Minimal Residual Disease (MRD) becomes important when it comes to determining treatment success and long-term outcomes in the complex field of cancer management. MRD, which is defined as a small number of cancer cells that remain in the body during or after treatment, is a prognostic marker that provides important information about the chance of a recurrence of the disease.

Remission, defined as the absence of detectable leukemia cells in the bone marrow, is a critical milestone for patients diagnosed with acute lymphoblastic leukemia (ALL). But the pursuit of total disease eradication goes beyond traditional diagnostic techniques. This is where MRD becomes extremely important.

The subtle remnants of residual disease that may be hiding in the biological landscape may go unnoticed by the traditional methods used to evaluate treatment response. Highly sensitive technologies, such as polymerase chain reaction (PCR) and flow cytometry, are used in MRD detection techniques to identify minimal leukemia cells present at levels that are undetectable by routine assessments. The capacity to identify these remaining cells allows for a more sophisticated comprehension of the effectiveness of treatment and the likelihood of disease recurrence.

MRD negativity following initial treatment in the context of ALL indicates a deeper degree of response. Individuals who attain MRD negativity exhibit a decreased likelihood of relapsing in contrast to those who maintain MRD. This differentiation assumes particular significance in directing treatment choices, molding post-remission tactics, and forecasting long-term survival results.

Beyond its predictive function, MRD is important because it can be used as a dynamic tool to customize treatment plans. When a patient tests positive for MRD, doctors may consider more intensive or focused treatment in an effort to eradicate any remaining disease and lower the chance of recurrence. However, MRD negativity minimizes the possibility of needless treatment-related toxicity by providing a path for the consideration of less aggressive therapeutic approaches.

The inclusion of MRD assessment in treatment algorithms is becoming more and more necessary as the medical community enters the era of precision medicine. A more individualized and successful therapeutic approach is made possible by the ability to further refine risk stratification by grouping patients according to their MRD status. The overarching objectives of maximizing treatment outcomes and minimizing side effects are in line with this personalized medicine strategy.

In light of this, the introduction of blinatumomab as a therapeutic ally becomes even more significant. Present at the annual meeting of the American Society of Hematology (ASH), the latest clinical trial results highlight how blinatumomab can improve outcomes for ALL patients who reach MRD negativity. The ability of the therapy to target disease residual at an undetectable level presents new opportunities for achieving long-term remission and higher rates of survival.

The implications of blinatumomab in the setting of MRD-negative ALL will be discussed in the following sections, along with the complex interactions that exist between this novel immunotherapy and the ever-changing minimal residual disease landscape.

Synopsis of Conventional Chemotherapy and Its Drawbacks

The cornerstone of cancer treatment, including the care of acute lymphoblastic leukemia (ALL), has long been standard chemotherapy. This traditional method uses cytotoxic agents that interrupt the cell cycle and obstruct cell division in order to destroy cancer cells that divide quickly. Chemotherapy has been very successful in causing remission, but there are a number of drawbacks that make alternative and supplemental treatment modalities necessary.

When treating ALL, the main objective of standard chemotherapy is to induce complete remission, which is defined as no longer having any detectable leukemia cells in the bone marrow. A combination of chemotherapeutic drugs are administered during this initial, frequently intense phase of treatment. The fact that a sizable percentage of patients experience remission is proof positive that this strategy works. Remission is not the end of the journey, though, as there is a significant chance of disease recurrence.

The fact that standard chemotherapy is not selective is one of its main drawbacks when treating ALL patients. Chemotherapeutic agents affect healthy, rapidly proliferating cells in addition to cancer cells. This indiscriminate attack on normal cells is a contributing factor to the widely recognized adverse effects of chemotherapy, which include fatigue, nausea, hair loss, and immunosuppression. When these adverse effects compound, the patient's quality of life and compliance with the treatment plan may be seriously jeopardized.

In addition, the problem of minimal residual disease (MRD) continues to be a crucial factor to take into account when using conventional chemotherapy. Even after remission, there is always a chance of a relapse because there are still leukemia cells present at levels that are not picked up by standard testing. It's possible that standard chemotherapy won't be able to completely eradicate these leftover cells, so finding new treatment approaches will be necessary to overcome this clinical obstacle.

Standard chemotherapy has significant limitations when treating adult patients with high-risk ALL, as there is a delicate balance between achieving remission and minimizing long-term toxicities. Because of the aggressive nature of the disease and the possibility of treatment-related complications, adult patients with ALL frequently face more difficult obstacles.

The development of immunotherapies and targeted therapies has provided a glimmer of hope in the fight for better treatment outcomes. Bispecific T-cell engager (BiTE) immunotherapy, such as blinatumomab, is a revolutionary treatment for ALL. Blinatumomab, in contrast to chemotherapy, works precisely by using the patient's immune system to target cancer cells specifically while preserving healthy tissues.

The shortcomings of conventional chemotherapy emphasize the critical need for novel and focused strategies that can increase therapeutic efficacy while reducing the side effects of conventional treatments. Because of blinatumomab's distinct mode of action and encouraging outcomes from clinical trials, there may be a way to get around MRD's drawbacks and improve the care that ALL patients receive.

The comparison with standard chemotherapy will shed light on the transformative potential of immunotherapeutic interventions in changing the treatment landscape for ALL, as we delve into the implications of blinatumomab in the following sections.

Blinatumomab: A Comprehensive Overview of Bispecific T-cell Engagers (BiTEs)

Blinatumomab is a leading agent in the dynamic field of cancer immunotherapy. It works by utilizing a special mechanism of action based on the idea of Bispecific T-cell Engagers (BiTEs). This novel strategy departs from established cancer therapies by leveraging the complex interactions between the immune system's powerful T cells and the cancerous cells typical of acute lymphoblastic leukemia (ALL).

The concept of Bispecific T-cell Engagers forms the basis of blinatumomab's mode of action. BiTEs are synthetic molecules with the extraordinary capacity to bind two distinct cell types—in this example, cancer cells and T cells—at the same time. This duality is a crucial characteristic that enables BiTEs to act as links between these two cell types, bringing them closer together for a focused and targeted immune response.

As a type of BiTE immunotherapy, blinatumomab is intended to activate T cells and direct their cytotoxic potential against cancer cells, especially those connected to ALL. Its structure consists of two different binding domains, one specific to binding to T cells that are CD3-positive and the other to B cells that are CD19-positive, a surface marker associated with some leukemia cells.

After being administered, blinatumomab searches for its two targets, cancer cells and T cells, throughout the bloodstream. These immune warriors are activated and primed for an attack when they bind to CD3 on T cells. Concurrently, the interaction with CD19 on cancerous cells acts as a marker, directing T cells to specifically locate and interact with leukemia cells. This dynamic interaction ultimately results in the death of the cancer cell by causing the release of cytotoxic substances such as granzymes and perfins.

The BiTE mechanism is elegant because it can get around the traditional need for antigen presentation. By virtue of its BiTE design, blinatumomab allows for a more direct and antigen-independent engagement than other immunotherapies that depend on the recognition of particular antigens expressed on the surface of cancer cells. This characteristic is especially helpful in the context of ALL, since targeted therapies may not always be successful due to the heterogeneous nature of leukemia cells.

The effects of blinatumomab's mode of action go beyond its ability to cause cancer cells to lyse directly. Blinatumomab stimulates a more comprehensive immune response by stimulating T cells and facilitating their interaction with cancer cells. Memory T cell proliferation is indicative of this immunomodulatory effect, which may provide a persistent anti-leukemic immune memory that prevents disease recurrence.

The positive safety profile seen in clinical trials is a result of the precision and specificity ingrained in the BiTE mechanism. Biniatumomab reduces the amount of off-target effects on healthy tissues by engaging T cells specifically with cancer cells. This makes it a less toxic therapeutic option than traditional chemotherapy.

Understanding the Bispecific T-cell Engager mechanism of blinatumomab opens up a promising avenue in the search for efficient and focused immunotherapies for ALL, as we will explore in more detail in the sections that follow. The combination of this novel strategy with the intricacies of leukemia biology could revolutionize cancer therapy and usher in a new age of precision medicine.

Blinatumomab's Mechanism of Action in Targeting Cancer Cells

Because it can coordinate a highly targeted and dynamic immune response against the malignant cells that are characteristic of Acute Lymphoblastic Leukemia (ALL), blinatumomab has demonstrated remarkable efficacy in targeting cancer cells. The accuracy of its mode of action is evidence of how cancer treatments are developing and how using the body's immune system to combat hematological malignancies is becoming increasingly important.

After being administered, blinatumomab travels through the bloodstream in search of T cells and cancer cells, which are its main targets. Because of its dual-binding domains, blinatumomab can interact with both types of cells at the same time, creating a bridge between the leukemia cells and the immune system. This ability is crucial for its therapeutic precision.

Blinatumomab's first binding domain is made specifically to bind to T cells that are CD3-positive. T cell surface markers like CD3 are easily identifiable, and when blinatumomab binds to them, a series of things happen. The T cells become primed for a heightened immune response against any perceived threat, including cancer cells that carry CD19 markers, as a result of this interaction.

Blindatumomab's second binding domain specifically targets B cells that are positive for CD19, a surface marker associated with some leukemia cells in ALL. This link acts as a homing mechanism, precisely directing the activated T cells toward the cancer cells. When blinatumomab interacts with T cells and cancer cells, it brings these cellular components closer together, allowing for precise and direct interactions.

The T cells use the CD19 marker to identify the leukemia cells, and once they do, they release granzymes and perforins, two powerful cytotoxic weapons. These cytotoxic chemicals pierce the membrane of cancer cells and cause apoptosis, or programmed cell death. Because of the blinatumomab's inherent selectivity, the outcome is the targeted destruction of the cancer cell while avoiding collateral damage to healthy tissues.

The immune system's guardians and the rogue cancer cells engage in a subtle dance during the dynamic interaction that blinatumomab orchestrates. This immunotherapeutic strategy promotes a more extensive immune response in addition to directly causing cancer cell lysis. Memory T cell proliferation is sparked by T cell activation, which may result in the formation of an immune memory reservoir that lasts longer than the duration of the current treatment. This immune memory serves as a watchful defender, ready to identify and neutralize any resurgence of leukemia cells and offer a persistent barrier against the illness's recurrence.

The mechanism of blinatumomab is antigen-independent, setting it apart from traditional immunotherapies that depend on the cancer cell surface's recognition of particular antigens. This characteristic is especially helpful in the context of ALL, since therapies based on the recognition of a single antigen may encounter difficulties due to the heterogeneity of leukemia cells.

The targeted approach of blinatumomab shows great therapeutic promise, which is further supported by the positive safety profile seen in clinical trials. Compared to conventional chemotherapy, the targeted interaction of T cells with cancer cells reduces the amount of collateral damage to healthy tissues and provides a therapeutic option with lower systemic toxicity.

The understanding of how blinatumomab targets cancer cells is profound, and as we explore its clinical implications in the following sections, it reveals a paradigm shift in the management of ALL. Targeted precision medicine is expected to revolutionize cancer treatment by combining the precision of this immunotherapeutic approach with the complex biology of leukemia.

Immunotherapy Developments in the Management of ALL

The development of immunotherapy, a ground-breaking strategy that uses the body's immune system to fight cancer, has revolutionized the treatment of acute lymphoblastic leukemia (ALL). A prominent player in this field is blinatumomab, a Bispecific T-cell Engager (BiTE), which stands out as a symbol of advancement in the fight against hematological malignancies and the move toward precision medicine.

Compared to conventional cancer treatments, which frequently use cytotoxic agents to target rapidly dividing cells—both malignant and healthy—immunotherapy is a paradigm shift. Rather, immunotherapy makes use of the immune system's complex machinery to enable it to identify and eradicate cancer cells with precision while protecting healthy tissues. This strategy represents a major advancement in the treatment of cancer and is in line with the overarching objective of attaining therapeutic efficacy with decreased toxicity.

Immunotherapy for ALL tackles long-standing issues brought on by the disease's heterogeneity and the possibility of a recurrence of minimal residual disease (MRD). The mechanism of action of blinatumomab, which is defined by its capacity to interact with both cancerous and T cells at the same time, is a prime example of the effectiveness of targeted immunotherapy in negotiating the intricate workings of leukemia biology.

Beyond blinatumomab, immunotherapy has evolved in the treatment of ALL; additional promising agents have added to the growing toolkit of precision medicine. For example, CAR-T (chimeric antigen receptor T-cell) therapy is another innovative immunotherapeutic strategy. Through genetic modification, a patient's own T cells can express receptors that specifically target leukemia-associated antigens as part of CAR-T therapy. These modified T cells have improved leukemia cell targeting and destruction once they are reinfused into the patient.

The FDA's approval of CAR-T therapy for the treatment of specific cases of relapsed or refractory B-cell ALL is indicative of the therapy's success. The individualized approach that immunotherapy brings to the treatment of ALL is highlighted by the customized nature of CAR-T therapy, which customizes interventions according to each patient's distinct biological profile.

Combination therapies are also showing promise; these approaches combine immunotherapy with conventional treatments or take advantage of the synergies between various immunotherapeutic agents. These strategies seek to improve treatment efficacy overall, reduce resistance mechanisms, and increase the range of patients who can benefit from immunotherapy.

Developments in immunotherapy have implications for survivorship and quality of life that go beyond clinical results in the treatment of ALL. Immunotherapy's lower systemic toxicity when compared to conventional chemotherapy means that patients will have a more bearable course of treatment. Immunotherapy patients may thus have fewer incapacitating side effects, improving their quality of life both during and after treatment.

Still, there are obstacles in the way of fully realizing immunotherapy's potential in ALL patients. Research is still ongoing to improve patient selection criteria and optimize treatment regimens, as well as to determine the cost and accessibility of these state-of-the-art treatments.

The convergence of scientific advancement and clinical implementation in the field of immunotherapy for ALL treatment is encouraging, as it points to a future in which targeted and personalized medicines will form the core of cancer treatment. The advancements of blinatumomab and its immunotherapeutic equivalents point the way toward a new chapter in the treatment of ALL, one in which the immune system's precision becomes a potent weapon against the unrelenting onslaught of leukemia.

Overview of the ECOG-ACRIN Cancer Research Group, an NCI-supported group

Multidisciplinary teams must work together in order to achieve scientific breakthroughs and advances in the field of cancer research. The Eastern Cooperative Oncology Group and the American College of Radiology Imaging Network (ECOG-ACRIN) Cancer Research Group, which are supported by the National Cancer Institute (NCI), become powerful forces that influence clinical trials and change the face of cancer treatment.

The ECOG-ACRIN Cancer Research Group is proof of the effectiveness of teamwork between eminent organizations, medical professionals, and researchers. ECOG and ACRIN are two prestigious organizations whose strengths are combined in this collaborative effort, which was founded with the goal of conducting innovative clinical trials in oncology. 2011 saw the merger of ECOG, which was founded in 1955, and ACRIN, which was founded in 1999, to form a collaborative platform for state-of-the-art cancer research.

Fundamentally, ECOG-ACRIN represents a dedication to quality in the planning, carrying out, and analyzing of clinical trials. Operating under the tenets of inclusivity, the cooperative group unites a network of more than 6000 oncologists from different specialties, including surgeons, radiation oncologists, medical oncologists, statisticians, and translational researchers. This multidisciplinary teamwork guarantees a thorough and multifaceted approach to managing the intricacies of cancer.

The ECOG-ACRIN Cancer Research Group's vital role in expanding our knowledge of cancer biology and treatment modalities is highlighted by the NCI's support of the group. The goal of ECOG-ACRIN is to conduct high-impact clinical trials that have the potential to change the standard of care for a variety of cancer types. This mission is in line with the NCI's, the main federal agency for cancer research and training.

Thanks to ECOG-ACRIN's strong organizational structure and infrastructure, the group is able to lead clinical trials for a variety of cancers, including hematological malignancies such as acute lymphoblastic leukemia (ALL). Launched in 2013, the clinical trial under discussion in relation to blinatumomab demonstrates the group's commitment to tackling important issues in cancer therapeutics.

Supported by the National Cancer Institute (NCI), this trial examined the effectiveness of blinatumomab in adults newly diagnosed with B-cell ALL. Although blinatumomab had previously demonstrated promise in the relapsed or refractory setting, this trial aimed to investigate its potential benefits as part of the first-line treatment regimen for adults with B-cell ALL. The trial's objectives were further complicated and relevant by focusing on patients who were in remission and minimal residual disease (MRD)-negative following initial chemotherapy regimens.

488 patients were enrolled in the trial, demonstrating a major cooperative effort to assemble a varied and representative study population. Notably, the results given at the annual meeting of the American Society of Hematology (ASH) shed light specifically on the subgroup of 224 patients who satisfied the requirements of being MRD-negative

and in remission following conventional initial chemotherapy.

The thorough approach typical of ECOG-ACRIN trials is reflected in the trial design, which includes elements like random assignment to treatment arms, the addition of maintenance chemotherapy, and the option for a bone marrow transplant based on clinical judgment.

The basic knowledge of the NCI-supported ECOG-ACRIN Cancer Research Group becomes essential to understanding the rigor and impact of the clinical trials influencing the future of cancer treatment as we go deeper into the trial results and their implications in the following sections. This research group's collaborative spirit is a beacon that points the scientific community in the direction of advancements that could potentially improve the lives of cancer patients all over the world.

Introduction and Planning of the Clinical Trial for Blinatumomab

The start of the blinatumomab clinical trial within the ECOG-ACRIN Cancer Research Group, which is supported by the NCI, was a significant turning point in the effort to rethink Acute Lymphoblastic Leukemia (ALL) treatment paradigms. This large-scale project, which was initiated in 2013, sought to investigate the possibility of using blinatumomab as the initial treatment for individuals who have been diagnosed with B-cell ALL. It offered a new way of tackling the difficulties caused by this aggressive hematological cancer.

The ECOG-ACRIN Cancer Research Group's multidisciplinary teams' combined expertise was reflected in the clinical trial's meticulous design. The primary objective of the trial was to determine whether blinatumomab is effective in treating patients who have undergone initial chemotherapy and are in remission. Additionally, the trial aimed to clarify the therapeutic nuances involved in integrating this novel immunotherapy into the frontline treatment regimen.

A sizable cohort of 488 participants was enrolled in the trial, demonstrating the cooperative efforts to assemble a varied and representative study population. A layer of precision was added to the trial's objectives by the strict patient selection criteria, which focused on patients who achieved remission and MRD negativity after standard initial chemotherapy regimens. This inclusivity was essential in guaranteeing the generalizability of the trial results to the larger population of adults with B-cell ALL.

The outcomes of patients receiving blinatumomab in addition to chemotherapy and those receiving chemotherapy alone could be robustly compared thanks to the random assignment of participants to different treatment arms, a feature of well-designed clinical trials. This randomized methodology reduces biases and enhances the dependability of the findings, offering a strong basis for clinical practice's use of evidence-based decision-making.

A maintenance chemotherapy phase was included in the trial to reflect the complexity of real-world scenarios and treatment courses. As part of an all-encompassing treatment plan, all participants underwent 2.5 years of maintenance chemotherapy, demonstrating the dedication to comprehending the long-term effects of blinatumomab. Furthermore, a personalized component was added to the trial by allowing certain patients to receive a bone marrow transplant at the discretion of their treating physicians. This allowed for the recognition of the variability in individual responses and clinical considerations.

The initiation and planning of this blinatumomab clinical trial demonstrated the dedication of the ECOG-ACRIN Cancer Research Group and its partners to advance the field of ALL treatment, and they went beyond simple scientific pursuits. The trial's emphasis on patients who tested negative for minimal residual disease (MRD) following initial chemotherapy highlighted the need for novel approaches to tackle the ongoing difficulties caused by MRD.

The trial offered a dynamic platform for continuous scientific inquiry and flexible learning as it went along. Through diligent data collection and ongoing patient outcome monitoring, the researchers were able to gain valuable insights into how ALL treatment is developing. The findings, which were presented at the annual meeting of the American Society of Hematology (ASH) in December 2022, would later influence the conversation regarding the place of blinatumomab in the paradigm for treating ALL.

A commitment to improving patient outcomes, clinical expertise, and scientific rigor are all combined in the design and implementation of the blinatumomab clinical trial. The ECOG-ACRIN Cancer Research Group's culture of collaboration paves the way for ground-breaking findings that could improve the quality of care for adults dealing with B-cell ALL.

Participant Enrollment Procedure and Selection Criteria

A clinical trial's dependability and success depend on how carefully the criteria for selecting participants are defined, striking a balance between generality and specificity. In the instance of the blinatumomab clinical trial run by the ECOG-ACRIN Cancer Research Group, which is supported by the

NCI, the participant selection criteria were carefully designed to address the particular difficulties presented by Acute Lymphoblastic Leukemia (ALL) and to look into the possible advantages of blinatumomab in a particular patient population.

A thorough evaluation of eligible participants was conducted before the trial's enrollment process began, underscoring the significance of having a varied and representative study cohort. Adults newly diagnosed with B-cell ALL were the only age group eligible for inclusion. This criterion guaranteed that the trial would concentrate on a particular patient subset dealing with the difficulties of a recent ALL diagnosis, enabling researchers to investigate the effectiveness of blinatumomab in the early stages of the disease.

A vital requirement for choosing participants was achieving remission after receiving standard first-line chemotherapy treatments. Achieving remission, defined by the absence of detectable leukemia cells in the bone marrow, was a prerequisite for inclusion in the trial. This criterion was designed to create a uniform participant base and baseline for disease control so that the effects of blinatumomab could be assessed on an even playing field.

The need for minimal residual disease (MRD) negativity added another level of specificity on top of remission. The absence of MRD, which indicates that there are no remaining traces of leukemia cells even at the molecular level, had to be demonstrated by the participants. This criterion focused on people with an even deeper level of treatment response, adding another degree of stringency to the participant selection process.

The justification for focusing on MRD-negative individuals stemmed from the recognition of the ongoing risk that minimal residual disease poses. The existence of MRD continued to be a possible marker for the recurrence of the disease even in cases where conventional evaluations showed remission. The trial focused on MRD-negative participants in order to investigate whether blinatumomab could improve outcomes even more in this particular subgroup, possibly changing the course of disease recurrence.

In addition to defining the traits of the eligible population, the participant selection criteria were created to be in line with the trial's overall objectives. The trial positioned the study at the nexus of early ALL treatment and the pursuit of long-term disease control by aiming to assess the effectiveness of blinatumomab in patients who had already experienced remission and MRD negativity.

The enrollment procedure itself followed a methodical approach, starting with the clinical centers that were involved in the process of identifying eligible individuals. Potential participants were informed about the trial and informed consent was obtained once they satisfied the rigorous criteria. Before deciding to participate in the trial, participants were guaranteed to be fully informed of its goals, possible risks, and benefits thanks to the informed consent process.

The criteria used to select participants and the enrollment procedure were not randomly chosen; rather, they were developed with a sophisticated awareness of the nuances involved in treating ALL. The trial sought to investigate a new aspect of blinatumomab's potential by concentrating on patients in remission who had MRD negativity. This focused on the drug's ability to prevent disease recurrence and lengthen the duration of remission.

Following clear participant selection guidelines became essential to the trial's overall success in terms of both internal and external validity. The rigorous enrollment procedure established the groundwork for a thorough examination of the effects of blinatumomab on the outcomes of adult B-cell ALL patients who had reached a particular degree of response to treatment.

Blinatumomab Improvements Overall Survival

One of the most important findings from the blinatumomab clinical trial, which was carried out by the ECOG-ACRIN Cancer Research Group with support from the NCI, was that patients with Acute Lymphoblastic Leukemia (ALL) who received blinatumomab as part of their post-remission therapy experienced a significant improvement in overall survival. The findings, which were presented at the annual meeting of the American Society of Hematology (ASH) in December 2022, represented a major advancement in the search for more effective treatment options for this aggressive hematological cancer.

The trial's key findings included a convincing illustration of how blinatumomab affected participants' long-term survival results. Overall survival rates were found to differ significantly between two cohorts: one that received chemotherapy alone, and the other that received blinatumomab and chemotherapy in combination. Compared to a 65% survival rate in the chemotherapy-alone group, 83% of patients in the blinatumomab group were still alive 3.5 years after starting post-remission therapy.

The trial's focus on patients who had achieved remission and minimal residual disease (MRD) negativity after standard initial chemotherapy regimens underscored the strategic approach to addressing the persistent risk of relapse in ALL, even in the absence of detectable leukemia cells. This remarkable difference in overall survival provided concrete evidence of the therapeutic efficacy of blinatumomab in the context of MRD-negative ALL.

The increase in overall survival that blinatumomab brought about both questioned accepted practices in healthcare and provided a glimmer of hope for patients attempting to navigate the intricacies of post-remission therapy. Leading the trial, Mayo Clinic physician Mark Litzow, M.D., noted that these outcomes "represent a new standard of care for individuals with MRD-negative ALL," emphasizing how blinatumomab can change the course of treatment by extending the duration of remission and lowering the risk of disease recurrence.

The longevity of the noted survival advantage prompted concerns regarding the long-term effects of adding blinatumomab to the list of post-remission treatment options. Reaching the 3.5-year mark was a significant turning point because it provided information about the long-term effects of blinatumomab on the course of ALL. The trial's long-lasting survival benefit suggested that blinatumomab might have a long-lasting impact on disease control as participants proceeded with their treatment.

The realization that undetectable minimal residual disease did not imply the absence of disease left further highlighted the significance of the overall survival improvement with blinatumomab. Richard Little, M.D., coauthor of the trial from the NCI's Division of Cancer Treatment and Diagnosis, stressed the significance of treating this extremely low level of disease that may be the cause of relapse. Blinatumomab proved to be a valuable strategic ally in the elimination of this elusive threat due to its accuracy in identifying leukemia cells that remained.

Wendy Stock, M.D. of the University of Chicago described the results as extremely exciting and impressive. The clinical implications of the improved overall survival extended beyond statistical measures, resonating with clinicians, researchers, and individuals facing the challenges of B-cell ALL. The results indicated that adding blinatumomab to post-remission therapy could be very beneficial for adult patients who achieve MRD-negative status following aggressive combination chemotherapy.

The conversation about blinatumomab's place in the continuum of care for ALL is gaining traction as the medical community struggles to comprehend the revolutionary implications of these trial results. This immunotherapeutic strategy is positioned as a cornerstone in the changing landscape of ALL treatment due to the higher overall survival rates and the trial's favorable blinatumomab safety profile.

The path taken by blinatumomab from trial design to the discovery of enhanced overall survival is indicative of both scientific rigor and a dedication to improving patient care. The 3.5-year survival milestone is evidence of blinatumomab's ability to raise the bar for patients starting the difficult journey of post-remission therapy for MRD-negative ALL and to redefine expectations.
A

Evaluation of Standard Chemotherapy in Separate

When compared to chemotherapy alone, the blinatumomab clinical trial, which was led by the ECOG-ACRIN Cancer Research Group and funded by the NCI, demonstrated the revolutionary potential of blinatumomab. A dramatic difference in the results was revealed by comparing these two treatment approaches, highlighting the paradigm-shifting effect of adding blinatumomab to the post-remission therapy for ALL.

The cohort treated with a combination of blinatumomab and chemotherapy was the clear winner in the trial's investigation of improved overall survival. When patients in the blinatumomab group were followed up for 3.5 years after starting post-remission therapy, their survival rate was 83%, which was significantly higher than the 65% survival rate of the chemotherapy-only group. The notable variation in survival results demonstrated the practical advantages of including blinatumomab in the treatment plan for patients with MRD-negative ALL.

Not only did the comparison with standard chemotherapy highlight the superiority of the blinatumomab-containing regimen, but it also disproved preconceived notions regarding the effectiveness of conventional treatments. Long regarded as the mainstay of ALL treatment, blinatumomab, an immunotherapeutic drug with a targeted mode of action, presented a serious challenge to chemotherapy.

Mark Litzow, M.D., of the Mayo Clinic, who led the trial, described these findings as a "new standard of care" for patients with MRD-negative ALL. The term "new standard of care" reverberated throughout the scientific community, indicating a paradigm shift in the field of therapy. The comparison demonstrated how blinatumomab has the potential to revolutionize ALL treatment, not just provide small improvements over the status quo.

The comparison went beyond survival results and explored tolerability and safety. Dr. Litzow stated that blinatumomab recipients did not experience any unanticipated side effects. This is consistent with earlier reports of the known adverse effects of blinatumomab, including fever, chills, headaches, infections, infusion-related reactions, and tremor. Another factor contributing to blinatumomab's appeal was its good safety record, which positioned it as a powerful therapeutic ally without sacrificing tolerability.

This comparison had an impact on treatment considerations that went beyond statistical measures and affected patient experience. The University of Chicago's Wendy Stock, M.D., expressed excitement about the results and what they might mean for B-cell ALL patients. Specifically, the results showed that adults who achieved

MRD-negative status following aggressive combination chemotherapy might greatly benefit from adding blinatumomab to post-remission therapy.

Intriguing questions concerning the future course of ALL treatment were also raised by the comparison of blinatumomab with conventional chemotherapy. The trial's design, which prioritized post-remission therapy, made people consider whether immunotherapy could be added earlier in the course of treatment. The trial results raised the question of whether immunotherapy—such as blinatumomab—should be taken into consideration earlier in the course of treatment, which Dr. Litzow acknowledged. This reflection indicated a break from sequential treatment approaches and suggested that treatment algorithms could be redesigned with the best interests of patients in mind.

In brief, the blinatumomab clinical trial's comparison with standard chemotherapy alone demonstrated not only the drug's superior overall survival but also its safety, tolerability, and potential to reshape the treatment landscape for MRD-negative ALL. The trial's conclusions encourage a reassessment of therapeutic norms, urging a move toward more targeted and precise approaches that may improve both the quality of life and efficacy for patients coping with the challenges of post-remission therapy for B-cell ALL.

Extended Results and MRD-Negative Individuals

The blinatumomab clinical trial, which was carried out by the ECOG-ACRIN Cancer Research Group, which is supported by the NCI, shed light on the benefits of immediate survival as well as long-term outcomes, especially for patients who were able to achieve Minimal Residual Disease

(MRD)-negative status. One of the most important aspects of the trial was the analysis of long-term effects, which provided insight into the long-term effects of blinatumomab in the complex field of treating acute lymphoblastic leukemia (ALL).

The trial specifically targeted MRD-negative patients who had completed standard initial chemotherapy regimens because it understood the ongoing difficulties caused by minimal residual disease, or the minute molecular remnants that, although conventional remission assessments may indicate a return of the disease, could still be a sign of it. As the trial participants progressed through their treatment, the evaluation of long-term results offered a comprehensive picture of blinatumomab's impact on the course of ALL after the initial post-remission stage.

The remarkable longevity of the survival benefit linked to blinatumomab was central to the long-term results. The 3.5-year mark represented a turning point, demonstrating the long-term effectiveness of blinatumomab in patients with MRD-negative status. The 83% overall survival rate for patients receiving chemotherapy and blinatumomab at this point in their treatment demonstrated their ability to withstand the risk of relapse. This long-lasting effect upended the traditional narrative surrounding ALL treatment and provided a ray of hope for those seeking both sustained disease control and remission.

Examining long-term results also led to reflection on the nature of minimal residual illness that is undetectable. Coauthor of the trial Richard Little, M.D., who works in NCI's Division of Cancer Treatment and Diagnosis, stressed that undetectable MRD did not mean no disease remained. This nuanced understanding emphasized the trial's importance in helping to understand the complexities of ALL and the importance of treating even the smallest amounts of residual disease that may act as a trigger for relapse.

The importance of long-term results was reflected in survival rates as well as in the observable enhancement of quality of life for patients with MRD-negative ALL. The findings indicated that blinatumomab, with its distinct mode of action that targets leukemia cells left behind, could not only increase survival time but also lessen the likelihood that the disease would recur.

The idea of long-term results also made people think about how treatment algorithms might be affected more broadly. The University of Chicago's Wendy Stock, M.D., emphasized the remarkable and thrilling outcomes, implying that the research showed noteworthy advantages for individuals attaining MRD-negative status following intense combination therapy. This viewpoint suggested that the treatment paradigm may change, with blinatumomab becoming an important component of the continuum of care for patients trying to deal with the long-term complications of ALL.

The emphasis on long-term outcomes indicates a forward-looking viewpoint as the medical community struggles with the complex ramifications of the blinatumomab trial. The long-lasting nature of the observed benefits instills hope in the ALL treatment landscape, questioning conventional wisdom and promoting a reassessment of the standards for individuals attaining MRD-negative status.

The blinatumomab clinical trial's investigation of long-term outcomes goes beyond survival statistics to examine the complexities of ongoing disease control and the subtleties of undetectable minimal residual disease. The results provide hope that blinatumomab may redefine not only the course of immediate treatment but also the long-term course of patients with MRD-negative ALL, helping them to balance the need for long-term disease control with remission.

FDA Approval and Treatment Guidelines.

The remarkable achievement of the blinatumomab clinical trial in enhancing overall survival for patients with Acute Lymphoblastic Leukemia (ALL) that was not positive for Minimal Residual Disease (MRD) marked a turning point in the path towards regulatory recognition and the development of treatment protocols. The Food and Drug Administration (FDA) approved blinatumomab for this particular patient population, marking a significant milestone that resulted from years of rigorous scientific inquiry and transformative clinical outcomes.

The FDA's approval, which came after strong trial results, signaled a significant change in the way that ALL is treated. After standard initial chemotherapy regimens, blinatumomab was first approved in 2018 for patients in remission but showing signs of cancer in follow-up testing (MRD-positive ALL). This approval has now been extended to include patients in remission with MRD-negative status. The extension of the approval signified an acknowledgment of blinatumomab's effectiveness in managing the distinct obstacles presented by residual disease, even in cases where traditional evaluations suggested remission.

The FDA's choice to approve blinatumomab for this particular group of patients highlighted the drug's therapeutic value as well as its potential to upend established treatment paradigms. The regulatory approval made blinatumomab a valuable tool in the fight against ALL, providing a focused strategy that sought both long-term disease control and remission, especially when combined with MRD-negative status.

The FDA's approval had a significant impact on the treatment guidelines' evolution. The University of Chicago's Wendy Stock, M.D., described the blinatumomab trial results as very remarkable and exciting. This sentiment struck a chord with clinicians navigating the complexities of treating patients with ALL as well as the scientific community. Due to the trial's success, treatment algorithms were reevaluated, and blinatumomab was given more careful thought for patients who achieved MRD-negative status during the post-remission phase.

Concerns concerning the wider integration of blinatumomab into the framework of ALL treatment strategies were also raised by the FDA approval and the changing treatment guidelines. After receiving approval from the FDA, blinatumomab became the go-to treatment for a particular patient population, shattering preconceived assumptions and prompting a reevaluation of the recommended course of treatment. The approval created a forum for debate about when immunotherapy should be started in the course of treatment and whether blinatumomab should be used sooner rather than later to optimize its potential advantages.

The FDA's approval and the updated treatment guidelines had an impact that went beyond just regulatory matters. The approval heralded a new chapter in ALL precision medicine, with blinatumomab at the forefront of highly focused immunotherapeutic approaches. The guidelines offered a roadmap for incorporating blinatumomab into the continuum of care, in line with the overarching objective of improving patient outcomes and reducing the risk of disease recurrence, to assist clinicians in navigating the changing landscape.

Blinatumomab's FDA approval for use in remission in patients with MRD-negative status signified a paradigm shift in the management of ALL. The regulatory acknowledgement advanced blinatumomab to the forefront of therapeutic approaches while also validating the trial's results. The FDA's decision has influenced the treatment guidelines, which have evolved to emphasize the need for a multifaceted strategy that goes beyond remission. This strategy emphasizes sustained disease control and the possibility that immunotherapy will redefine expectations for patients navigating the challenges of post-remission therapy for MRD-negative ALL.

Blinatumomab Approval for MRD-Positive ALL In 2018

The Food and Drug Administration (FDA) approved blinatumomab in 2018, which was a revolutionary development in the treatment of acute lymphoblastic leukemia

(ALL). This achievement was especially noteworthy because it gave regulatory recognition to blinatumomab's effectiveness in treating a particular patient subset: those in remission who, upon follow-up testing, showed evidence of cancer (known as Minimal Residual Disease (MRD)-positive ALL).

One notable feature of blinatumomab, a bispecific T-cell engager (BiTE) immunotherapy, is its ability to bind to both cancer cells and T cells at the same time. This helps the immune system recognize and eliminate remaining leukemia cells. After its first treatment, blinatumomab was positioned as a groundbreaking medication for patients with MRD-positive ALL thanks to the FDA's approval in 2018.

This regulatory approval was the result of numerous clinical trials and a strong body of evidence demonstrating blinatumomab's effectiveness in treating MRD-positive ALL.

The FDA's decision highlighted blinatumomab's therapeutic impact as well as its potential to redefine treatment paradigms by focusing on residual disease, which may go undetected in more conventional assessments.

With its approval in 2018, the treatment of ALL underwent a paradigm shift as established norms were challenged and the significance of treating MRD to prevent disease recurrence was emphasized. Due to the increased risk of relapse for those in remission who had MRD-positive status, the approval of blinatumomab represents a significant advancement in the search for better outcomes for this particular patient population.

The way blinatumomab worked, bringing T cells up close to cancer cells, demonstrated a precision-oriented strategy that set it apart from traditional chemotherapy. The approval was in line with the larger trend in cancer treatment toward precision medicine and suggested a move toward more specialized and focused therapeutic interventions.

In addition to providing a novel therapeutic option, the approval of blinatumomab for MRD-positive ALL in 2018 set off a chain reaction within the scientific and medical communities. With this new weapon in their toolbox, clinicians could potentially change the course of disease management for patients with MRD-positive ALL and address the ongoing challenge of residual disease.

The approval also sparked conversations about incorporating blinatumomab into the treatment regimens that are currently in place. The results are exciting and impressive, according to Wendy Stock, M.D. of the University of Chicago, indicating a reevaluation of therapeutic norms. The FDA's approval opened the door for discussions regarding when blinatumomab should be used in the treatment plan and whether it could change the course of the post-remission phase.

Blinatumomab, the first immunotherapy approved by the FDA for treating MRD-positive ALL, established a standard for subsequent advancements in the treatment of leukemia. It emphasized how critical it is to address the minute molecular traces that may indicate an underlying risk of relapse in addition to attaining remission. With its approval, blinatumomab became a cornerstone in the treatment of ALL, representing the promise of precision medicine to enhance outcomes for patients dealing with the challenges of post-remission therapy.

Treatment Guidelines and the Effects of Trial Results.

The medical community has been greatly impacted by the trial results of blinatumomab in the treatment of Acute Lymphoblastic Leukemia (ALL), with significant implications for recommended courses of care. The revolutionary effect of blinatumomab on overall survival has sparked a reassessment of current paradigms and discussions about how these findings should guide and reshape treatment guidelines, especially in the context of Minimal Residual Disease (MRD)-negative ALL.

A principal implication is that it calls into question the established order of treatment modalities in the post-remission stage. The trial's success was reported at the annual meeting of the American Society of

Hematology (ASH) in December 2022. It showed that when blinatumomab was added to chemotherapy, overall survival was significantly higher than when chemotherapy was used alone. The conventional use of chemotherapy as the only accepted standard of care in this situation is called into question by the notable improvement in the results.

The implications dive into the subtleties of long-term disease control, going beyond the immediate benefits to survival. The results, according to blinatumomab trial leader Mark Litzow, M.D., "represent a new standard of care for individuals with MRD-negative ALL." This statement has significant implications for treatment guidelines as it signals a shift from previous approaches and calls for a more targeted, nuanced strategy in the post-remission landscape.

The trial results have also spurred debate regarding when immunotherapy should be added to a patient's course of treatment. The idea of introducing blinatumomab earlier in the therapeutic regimen calls into question the sequential order of interventions. Since chemotherapy did not help many of the patients who were initially enrolled in the trial achieve complete remission, Dr. Litzow acknowledged that this raised the question of whether immunotherapy, such as blinatumomab, should be considered earlier in the course of treatment. This thought encourages a proactive approach to immunotherapy by introducing a dynamic shift in the temporal dimension of treatment guidelines.

The lack of unanticipated side effects documented in the trial adds to blinatumomab's safety profile and makes it an attractive addition to treatment protocols. The well-known and controllable side effects of blinatumomab include fever, chills, headaches, infections, infusion-related reactions, and tremor. The positive safety profile reduces worries about excessive toxicity and makes it more feasible to incorporate blinatumomab into standard protocols.

The University of Chicago's Wendy Stock, M.D., expressed excitement about the findings, highlighting that they point to important advantages for adults who receive aggressive combination chemotherapy and become MRD-negative. This opinion highlights how blinatumomab has the potential to change treatment protocols and patient expectations for MRD-negative ALL patients, as well as to increase survival and establish itself as a pillar of the continuum of care.

Beyond statistical measures, the trial results have far-reaching implications for treatment guidelines that are ingrained in clinical decision-making processes. The changing environment demands that therapeutic standards be reevaluated, pushing medical professionals to adopt a more complex, individualized strategy. Blinatumomab stands out as a precision medicine lighthouse, upending the established order and providing a revolutionary change in the way ALL is treated after remission as the medical community struggles with these implications.

The results of the blinatumomab trial have significant effects on treatment recommendations, questioning accepted wisdom and supporting a more focused, flexible strategy in the post-remission stage of ALL. The addition of blinatumomab to treatment guidelines not only denotes better results but also a significant advancement in precision medicine, establishing a standard for the deliberate inclusion of immunotherapeutic interventions in the all-encompassing management of ALL.

The Regulatory Environment and Upcoming Issues

The success of the blinatumomab clinical trial in improving outcomes for patients with Acute Lymphoblastic Leukemia (ALL) that is not associated with Minimal Residual Disease (MRD) has significant implications for the regulatory environment and provides insight into future factors that may shape the course of ALL treatment. Thoughts regarding more extensive approvals, combination treatments, and improved patient stratification become more prominent as the regulatory environment changes in reaction to revolutionary clinical outcomes.

The trial findings, which demonstrate blinatumomab's effectiveness in patients with MRD-negative status, may impact regulatory choices outside the parameters of the medication's original approval. Based on the strong data from the trial, the Food and Drug Administration (FDA), which first approved blinatumomab in 2018 for patients with MRD-positive ALL, may now consider extending its approval to MRD-negative patients. With this addition, blinatumomab would be even more positioned as a useful and essential weapon in the arsenal against ALL.

The trial has shown that blinatumomab has a good safety profile, which is an important factor in regulatory evaluations. The medication shows itself as a well-tolerated addition to the treatment options, with no unexpected side effects reported. Its favorable safety record supports its current status and creates opportunities for regulatory conversations about its use in larger patient populations—possibly including older and pediatric patients.

In order to maximize treatment outcomes, future considerations also explore the possibility of combining blinatumomab with other targeted therapies. The trial results highlight the effectiveness of blinatumomab when combined with chemotherapy, but they also raise questions about possible synergy with other novel agents. Current research examining the use of blinatumomab in conjunction with targeted treatments such as inotuzumab may offer important new perspectives on the viability and advantages of these multifaceted strategies. These factors might open the door for regulatory reviews of combination treatments, which might completely change how ALL patients are treated.

Future considerations must include patient stratification based on particular genetic and molecular traits. The trial emphasizes the significance of customizing treatments to individual disease profiles by focusing on MRD-negative patients following standard initial chemotherapy regimens. Optimizing the use of blinatumomab and other emerging therapies may require careful consideration of how to refine patient stratification strategies as the regulatory landscape changes. Regulations may be influenced by precision medicine techniques, which pinpoint the populations most benefited by particular therapies. This would guarantee focused and efficient interventions.

The efficacy of blinatumomab in the context of MRD-negative patients encourages research into the treatment of other hematological cancers. Regulatory considerations might encompass the exploration of blinatumomab's effectiveness in various settings, thereby expanding its influence to encompass a wide range of patient demographics. This development may establish blinatumomab as a flexible immunotherapeutic tool with wider applications in hematology, in addition to its role as a transformative agent in ALL.

Collaboration between regulatory agencies, researchers, and pharmaceutical companies becomes essential as the regulatory landscape changes in response to the blinatumomab trial results. In the future, it will be important to create an atmosphere that supports patient-centered care, fosters innovation, and expedites approvals based on strong clinical evidence. The triumph of blinatumomab offers a guide for subsequent undertakings in precision medicine, wherein customized treatments based on the molecular details of every patient's ailment assume a central role.

The blinatumomab trial results have created a dynamic regulatory landscape and future considerations that could potentially change the way that ALL is treated. The legacy of blinatumomab serves as a catalyst for a new era in precision medicine, paving the way for more efficient and customized interventions in the field of hematological malignancies as regulatory bodies negotiate the challenges of increasing approvals, investigating combination therapies, improving patient stratification, and considering broader applications.

Patient Views of Blinatumomab Therapy

The effects of blinatumomab on patients with acute lymphoblastic leukemia (ALL) go beyond clinical measures and into the domains of personal experiences, aspirations, and viewpoints. Gaining insight into the patient's experience and viewpoints regarding blinatumomab treatment is crucial in order to comprehend the transformative nature of this immunotherapeutic approach and its importance for individuals coping with the intricacies of ALL.

When an individual is diagnosed with ALL, they may experience a range of emotions related to treatment, including fear, uncertainty, and hope. With its unique mode of action and encouraging clinical outcomes, blinatumomab has become a ray of hope for a great number of patients. Patients looking for alternatives to traditional chemotherapy that are as effective but less toxic find great appeal in the idea of a treatment that not only targets the cancer cells directly but also leverages the immune system's strength.

The desire for better quality of life both during and after therapy is frequently highlighted in patient perspectives regarding blinatumomab treatment. Despite their effectiveness, traditional chemotherapy regimens are linked to a number of side effects that can seriously interfere with a patient's day-to-day activities. The trial findings regarding blinatumomab's favorable safety profile point to an improved quality of treatment outcome. Patients express gratitude for a treatment option that not only shows promise in the fight against ALL but also lessens the impact of side effects associated with treatment, providing a sense of normalcy despite the difficulties associated with fighting cancer.

Patients and their families experience a palpable sense of optimism as a result of the trial's demonstrable improvement in overall survival. People are motivated to overcome the challenges of treatment with resiliency and determination by the possibility of living a longer and healthier life after remission. Patient viewpoints frequently highlight the significant influence that survival results have on their general well-being, which inspires them to take on the challenges that ALL presents.

It takes both mental and physical toughness to navigate the complexities of ALL treatment. Regarding blinatumomab treatment, patient perspectives frequently stress the significance of maintaining mental and emotional health throughout the therapeutic process. Patients have a more positive emotional experience as a result of blinatumomab's decreased side effects and enhanced tolerability, which helps them maintain a higher quality of life while undergoing treatment and cultivates hope for the future.

The effects of blinatumomab on patients with ALL become significantly impacted by patient involvement and advocacy. People's narratives about their experiences with blinatumomab add to the expanding body of patient-centered knowledge as they are shared. By fostering a sense of community among those facing similar challenges, this shared knowledge empowers patients to make informed decisions about their treatment and elevates the voice of patients in the larger conversation surrounding the management of ALL.

Finally, patient viewpoints regarding blinatumomab therapy highlight the complex effects of this immunotherapeutic strategy on the lives of ALL patients. Beyond its ability to treat medical conditions effectively, blinatumomab appeals to patients as a sign of hope, a way to lead a better life, and a boost to their emotional health. The opinions of patients provide an essential compass, directing the course of ALL treatment towards more patient-centric, individualized, and transformative interventions as the medical community continues to investigate and improve therapeutic approaches.

Life Quality and Survivability

When it comes to the treatment of Acute Lymphoblastic Leukemia (ALL), the introduction of blinatumomab has had a significant impact on survivorship experiences and quality of life for those battling this hematological cancer, in addition to improving survival rates. Beyond the short-term clinical measures, the addition of blinatumomab to treatment approaches has reshaped the characteristics of survivorship, forming a story that prioritizes improved quality of life, lessened treatment-related stress, and a fresh outlook on life after ALL.

In the context of cancer survivorship, quality of life—a complex concept that includes physical, emotional, and social well-being—takes on a greater significance. The unique way that blinatumomab targets cancer cells while reducing the negative effects of conventional chemotherapy is consistent with the desire for a higher standard of living. Patients receiving blinatumomab treatment frequently report fewer and milder side effects, which enhances their quality of life on a daily basis while they pursue treatment.

One of the most important factors in improving the quality of life for patients treated with blinatumomab is the sparing effect on bone marrow, which is frequently the site of collateral damage in conventional chemotherapy. Conventional chemotherapy may cause myelosuppression, which would impair the body's capacity to make vital blood components. However, the targeted action of blinatumomab reduces these systemic effects, enabling patients to continue producing red blood cells and having a stronger immune system. For survivors, this preservation of hematopoietic function means less fatigue, more energy, and an overall better sense of physical well-being.

Survivors are deeply affected emotionally by the idea of a treatment that is more tolerable and has fewer side effects. The more favorable side effect profile of blinatumomab helps to lessen the emotional toll of cancer treatment, which is often made worse by the difficulties presented by conventional therapies. Lessening the distress associated with treatment allows survivors to concentrate on starting over after therapy, which builds emotional toughness and enhances the survivorship experience.

The effect of blinatumomab on quality of life also affects social aspects of survivorship. In spite of the difficulties of fighting cancer, survivors are able to participate more fully in social activities due to the lighter treatment load. Retaining social ties and engaging in community life are essential aspects of being a survivor, and blinatumomab's ability to reduce treatment-related interruptions helps survivors recover their social identities outside of the context of cancer.

In the case of blinatumomab, survival goes beyond the end of active treatment. The clinical trial's improved overall survival rates, which attest to blinatumomab's sustained efficacy, provide survivors hope for a future with wider possibilities. The possibility of a longer survival not only gives survivors hope, but it also gives them the drive to plan ahead and work toward long-term objectives, be they social goals, professional goals, or significant contributions to their communities.

In summary, the effects of blinatumomab on the quality of life and survivability experiences of ALL patients go beyond conventional measures of treatment efficacy. Blindatumomab is a transformative agent that contributes to the creation of a more positive and holistic survivorship narrative by reducing the burdens associated with treatment, maintaining physical and mental well-being, and opening new opportunities for survivors. The potential for blinatumomab to become a cornerstone in fostering a thriving survivorship experience for individuals overcoming the challenges of ALL is highlighted by the intersection of improved survival outcomes and enhanced quality of life, which is driven by the ongoing advancements in precision medicine within the medical community.

Answering Frequently Asked Questions and Illusions

In the medical community as well as among patients, the introduction of blinatumomab as an immunotherapeutic option for Acute Lymphoblastic Leukemia (ALL) has generated interest and optimism. Like any novel treatment, there are some common misconceptions and worries that need to be carefully considered. It is imperative to tackle these concerns in order to promote well-informed decision-making, build patient confidence, and enable the smooth assimilation of blinatumomab into the therapeutic regimen.

One frequent worry is about blinatumomab's safety profile. Although the results of the clinical trials have shown a good safety profile with no unexpected side effects, concerns might still exist because of the novel way in which the drug works. In order to address this issue, detailed information regarding the particular side effects of blinatumomab, including fever, chills, headaches, infections, tremor, and infusion-related reactions, must be made available. Safety concerns are reduced by highlighting the controllable nature of these side effects and the proactive monitoring techniques implemented during treatment.

There may also be misconceptions regarding the effectiveness of blinatumomab in comparison to conventional chemotherapy. Encouraging medical professionals and patients to learn about the trial findings—which demonstrated increased overall survival when blinatumomab was used—is crucial to eradicating any concerns that immunotherapy might be less successful than traditional therapies. It helps to set realistic expectations and ensures appropriate patient selection to communicate clearly about the specific patient population for whom blinatumomab has demonstrated significant benefits, especially those with Minimal Residual Disease (MRD)-negative status following initial chemotherapy.

Another factor to take into account could be worried about blinatumomab's availability and accessibility. In order to allay these worries, details regarding the drug's approval status, possible incorporation into treatment guidelines, and continuous initiatives to make cutting-edge therapies available to a larger patient base must be provided. Emphasizing the partnerships among regulatory agencies, medical professionals, and pharmaceutical firms to expedite the acquisition of blinatumomab serves to reaffirm the dedication to providing innovative therapies to individuals who could stand to gain from them.

One myth that could surface has to do with the requirement for bone marrow transplants in addition to blinatumomab therapy. It helps to clear up any misunderstandings regarding the treatment strategy to clarify that the trial's results were presented without requiring bone marrow transplants and that individual doctors made decisions about such procedures. This assurance is essential to presenting a complex picture of blinatumomab's place in the larger therapeutic context.

Financial concerns regarding new treatments such as blinatumomab are not uncommon. In order to allay these worries, details regarding insurance coverage, possible financial aid programs, and continuous initiatives to make patients' access to cutting-edge treatments affordable must be provided. Promoting equitable healthcare requires making sure that access to transformative therapies is not impeded by financial concerns.

Clearing up common questions and misunderstandings about blinatumomab is essential to creating an open and encouraging healthcare environment. Clear communication that is based on data from studies is essential for removing doubts and fostering confidence in both patients and healthcare professionals. By taking these issues head-on, the medical community can create the conditions for a more knowledgeable, self-assured, and cooperative approach to blinatumomab integration into the changing landscape of ALL treatment.

Unanswered Clinical Trial Questions

In addition to presenting strong evidence of blinatumomab's effectiveness and transformative potential in the treatment of acute lymphoblastic leukemia (ALL), the blinatumomab clinical trial has raised a number of unanswered questions that highlight the challenges associated with managing ALL and suggest areas for future research.

A critical question that emerged from the clinical trial concerns the best time to administer immunotherapy, specifically blinatumomab, over the course of treatment. The trial findings demonstrated how, following initial chemotherapy, people with Minimal Residual Disease (MRD)-negative status had better overall survival rates. The question of whether immunotherapy should be started earlier in the course of treatment is still relevant and complex, though. Examining the possible advantages of starting blinatumomab earlier in the course could shed light on how it functions as a front-line or adjuvant therapy, changing the way that ALL treatment is administered over time.

One more important question concerns blinatumomab's possible synergy with other targeted therapies. Although the trial concentrated on the use of blinatumomab in conjunction with chemotherapy, research is still ongoing to determine whether it is compatible with and more effective when used in conjunction with other novel agents. Current trials are being conducted to better understand the complex interactions between targeted therapies and immunotherapy. One such trial is testing blinatumomab in combination with inotuzumab and chemotherapy. Deciphering these synergies may lead to improved combination strategies, which would further improve outcomes for ALL patients.

It's still unclear how blinatumomab works in certain subsets of ALL patients. The clinical trial demonstrated notable advantages in terms of overall survival and was centered on MRD-negative patients following initial chemotherapy. It is imperative to further investigate its effectiveness in various genetic and molecular subtypes of ALL. In order to address the inherent heterogeneity within the ALL patient population, a more personalized and effective approach may be achieved by customizing treatment strategies based on specific disease characteristics.

Research on the effects of blinatumomab on sustained remission and their long-term durability is ongoing. Even though the trial showed an improvement in overall survival, more extended follow-up data must be examined in order to determine how long-lasting these results will be. Examining whether blinatumomab helps maintain disease control over time by averting relapses enhances our comprehension of its function in the continuum of care for ALL.

In addition, questions regarding blinatumomab's possible combination with other cutting-edge immunotherapies are raised by the idea of including it in treatment guidelines. Examining the interoperability and synergies between various modalities may reveal new paths toward improving therapeutic efficacy and increasing treatment options for patients with ALL as immunotherapy progresses.

To sum up, the blinatumomab clinical trial has not only provided answers to important queries, but it has also prompted fresh ones that highlight how dynamic ALL research is. The unanswered concerns about the best time to start immunotherapy, how to work in conjunction with targeted therapies, whether a treatment is effective in a particular subgroup, how long the effects last, and how to combine treatments show the difficulties that still need to be overcome and the directions that need to be taken in order to provide more accurate, efficient, and customized care for patients dealing with the complex nature of ALL. These questions act as compass points for future research, pointing the scientific and medical communities in the direction of a better understanding and more sophisticated approaches to better outcomes for ALL patients.

Examining the Integration of Early Immunotherapy

Especially when it comes to treating Acute Lymphoblastic Leukemia (ALL), the investigation of early immunotherapy integration marks a paradigm change in the way this intricate hematological cancer is treated. The outcomes of the blinatumomab clinical trial have provoked a thorough investigation into the possible advantages and difficulties of starting immunotherapy earlier in the course of treatment, upending established beliefs and creating opportunities to redefine the temporal dynamics of managing ALL.

Immunotherapies such as blinatumomab were previously only used in certain stages of ALL, such as following an initial chemotherapy regimen if there was minimal residual disease (MRD) positivity. The clinical trial results, which show that patients with MRD-negative status had an improved overall survival rate, prompt interesting queries regarding the best time to start immunotherapy. By utilizing the immune system's potential at an earlier stage of the disease process, investigating the integration of blinatumomab earlier in the course of treatment holds the promise of improving therapeutic outcomes.

The potential to more effectively eradicate residual disease is a crucial component of the integration of early immunotherapy. The trial demonstrated that a low level of disease is still responsible for relapse and that undetectable MRD does not imply the absence of disease. With its focused mode of action, blinatumomab can be started early and proactively treat this residual disease, stopping its progression and decreasing the chance of relapse. This proactive strategy is in line with the main objective of helping ALL patients experience more profound and long-lasting responses.

Examining the integration of early immunotherapy also prompts questions about how this might affect treatment toxicity. Even though traditional chemotherapy is effective, it has a lot of side effects that can be difficult for patients to deal with, especially over time. It may be possible to minimize cumulative chemotherapy exposure by introducing immunotherapy earlier in the treatment continuum, which would lessen the overall treatment burden. This takes into account the overarching goal of enhancing the standard of living for ALL patients by reducing the side effects of conventional treatment.

The investigation into the integration of early immunotherapy goes beyond blinatumomab and takes a more comprehensive view of immunotherapeutic approaches. Novel immunotherapies with unique mechanisms of action are developing as the field develops, offering chances for early integration in various stages of ALL. It is crucial to conduct early treatment phase investigations into the safety, effectiveness, and compatibility of various immunotherapeutic modalities in order to optimize therapeutic approaches and customize interventions to the specific needs of each patient.

Thorough research is required to address issues related to the integration of early immunotherapy, such as patient selection criteria, potential resistance mechanisms, and best combination strategies. To overcome these obstacles, scientists, physicians, and pharmaceutical companies must work together to create thorough studies that clarify the complexities of early immunotherapy integration. Furthermore, strong translational research initiatives are essential to clarify the immunological environment of ALL at various stages, directing the creation of focused and efficient early immunotherapeutic strategies.

To sum up, investigating the integration of early immunotherapy is a revolutionary investigation that could change the course of ALL treatment. The potential to utilize immunotherapies such as blinatumomab in earlier phases of the disease creates new opportunities to attain more profound and long-lasting responses, reduce side effects from treatment, and enhance the overall quality of life for patients with ALL. In the ongoing pursuit of more efficient, focused, and patient-centered approaches to managing ALL, early immunotherapy integration is a dynamic and promising avenue for precision medicine advancement.

Possible Blends with Personalized Medicines

The treatment landscape for acute lymphoblastic leukemia (ALL) is changing, and this has sparked interest in investigating possible combos between targeted therapies and blinatumomab. The outcomes of the clinical trials, which demonstrate the effectiveness of blinatumomab when combined with chemotherapy, have made it possible to look into potential synergistic interactions with additional targeted agents. By utilizing complementary mechanisms of action, improving treatment approaches, and tackling the molecular complexity of ALL, this investigation marks a significant advancement in the field.

Combining blinatumomab with targeted therapies that specifically target the genetic and molecular abnormalities common in ALL subtypes is one line of inquiry. One noteworthy effort is the combination of blinatumomab and inotuzumab, a targeted therapy approved for B-cell precursor ALL that has relapsed or is refractory. Such combinations seek to optimize therapeutic efficacy by concurrently targeting distinct pathways implicated in ALL, potentially overcoming resistance mechanisms and providing a more comprehensive approach to disease management.

Beyond the context of conventional chemotherapy, possible combinations with targeted therapies are being investigated. A promising area of research is blinatumomab's compatibility with small molecule inhibitors and other newly developed targeted agents. Combining blinatumomab with other small molecules that target particular genetic mutations linked to ALL or signaling pathways may result in a multimodal attack on cancer cells. This strategy fits in with the larger oncology trend toward precision medicine, which customizes care to the distinct molecular features of each patient's illness.

Combinations that could work include immunomodulatory drugs, which can improve the immune system's reaction to blinatumomab. Immunomodulators that maximize the potential of immune cells, like checkpoint inhibitors or cytokine therapies, have shown promise in treating specific cancers. Examining their function in conjunction with blinatumomab seeks to enhance the immune response against ALL cells, thereby broadening the scope of immunotherapy and enhancing its influence on disease management.

One of the challenges linked to possible combinations is figuring out the best dosing, sequencing, and safety profiles for these multi-agent regimens. When developing combination therapies, it's important to take into account possible overlapping toxicities and come up with ways to reduce side effects. Furthermore, careful preclinical and translational research is needed to understand the mechanisms underlying the synergy or antagonistic effects of blinatumomab with targeted agents in order to effectively inform clinical trial design.

Investigating possible pairings with targeted therapies fits in with the larger oncology trend of developing more individualized and accurate treatment plans. The molecular heterogeneity of ALL calls for creative approaches that transcend universal protocols. Researchers hope to leverage the therapeutic benefits of each modality and create a synergistic effect that improves overall treatment outcomes by combining blinatumomab with targeted therapies.

In this field, future directions include finding biomarkers that can direct patient selection for particular regimens and broadening the range of combination strategies. With a deeper understanding of the molecular landscape of ALL, targeted therapies hold great promise for changing the paradigm of care. Researcher, pharmaceutical, and regulatory agency collaboration is essential to moving these combinations from preclinical studies to clinical practice.

A vibrant and promising area of research in ALL is the investigation of possible pairings between blinatumomab and targeted therapies. These combinations, which are based on precision medicine principles, are intended to customize treatments to the specific molecular features of each patient's illness, thereby promoting a new era of more efficient, focused, and patient-centered approaches to the management of ALL.

Professional Opinion on Trial Results

The medical community has responded significantly to the release of trial results regarding blinatumomab's effectiveness in treating Acute Lymphoblastic Leukemia (ALL). The opinions expressed by experts highlight the immunotherapeutic approach's transformative potential. A nuanced understanding of the trial results, implications for managing ALL, and the wider implications for advancing treatment paradigms in hematological malignancies can be gained from the expert perspectives and insights shared.

Hematology and oncology experts have praised the trial results as a historic discovery that will change the way patients with ALL are treated. Experts have expressed profound resonance with the observed improvement in overall survival, especially in patients with Minimal Residual Disease (MRD)-negative status following initial chemotherapy, which has signaled a paradigm shift in the way clinicians approach post-remission therapy. The importance of these findings has been underlined by many, who point out that they not only increase survival rates but also refute accepted wisdom regarding the best time to introduce immunotherapies like blinatumomab into the treatment regimen.

Regarding the trial results, expert opinions frequently draw attention to the wider ramifications for immunotherapy's use in treating ALL. The efficaciousness of blinatumomab as a bispecific T-cell engager (BiTE) has initiated conversations regarding the possibility of analogous immunotherapeutic strategies in managing the intricacies of hematological cancers. Scholars recognize that blinatumomab has a distinct mode of action that involves both T cells and cancer cells at the same time. They also emphasize the drug's wider relevance in the developing field of immunotherapy for ALL and possibly other hematologic malignancies.

The trial's conclusions have also made people think about how we currently understand MRD, or minimal residual disease, and how it relates to relapse. The trial results highlight the significance of eliminating even the lowest levels of disease to prevent relapse, and experts stress the importance of understanding that undetectable MRD does not equate to the absence of disease. In expert discussions, this nuanced view of MRD and its function in formulating treatment strategies has taken center stage, directing future thinking regarding risk assessment and therapeutic interventions.

Notwithstanding the encouraging results, experts recognize the difficulties and unresolved issues raised by the trial. Experts predict that areas such as the exploration of combinations with other targeted therapies, the possibility of integrating blinatumomab at earlier stages of treatment, and the development of nuanced patient selection criteria will drive future research endeavors. These ongoing investigations highlight how dynamic hematology and oncology research is and how important it is for the medical community to constantly adapt treatment plans in light of new findings.

Expert opinions frequently address broader implications for patient care and outcomes, going beyond the scientific and clinical aspects. Experts are thinking about how the trial's higher overall survival rates might affect patients' lives and stress the value of survivorship experiences and overall quality of life. Expert discourse should include discussions on the integration of blinatumomab into treatment guidelines, possible modifications to standard chemotherapy regimens, and the changing landscape of ALL management.

Expert opinions on the trial results, in summary, demonstrate a shared understanding of blinatumomab's revolutionary influence on the field of treating acute lymphoblastic leukemia. The trial's findings have spurred deliberative debates, brought up significant issues, and laid the groundwork for future developments in our knowledge of and approach to treating ALL. Expert opinions not only add to the body of knowledge but also influence the direction of future studies, clinical procedures, and the medical community's general strategy for treating hematologic malignancies.

Using Blinatumomab in Clinical Settings

A significant change in the field of clinical practice has been brought about by the ground-breaking trial results regarding the effectiveness of blinatumomab in treating Acute Lymphoblastic Leukemia (ALL). As specialists examine the ramifications of these findings, the incorporation of blinatumomab into standard clinical practice becomes apparent as a crucial factor, igniting conversations about the best way to choose patients, the best order to administer treatments, and the overall effect on ALL care.

Improving patient selection criteria is a crucial part of using blinatumomab in clinical practice. Trial participants with ALL who, following initial chemotherapy, achieved Minimal Residual Disease (MRD)-negative status demonstrated notable improvements in overall survival. It is now the responsibility of clinicians to determine which patient subgroup will benefit the most from blinatumomab, taking into account variables like disease characteristics, genetic profiles, and response to initial treatments. This individualized approach, which bases interventions on the particulars of each patient's illness, is consistent with the larger oncology trend toward precision medicine.

Another important factor in clinical practice is the order in which blinatumomab is administered within the treatment continuum. Although post-remission therapy was the main focus of the trial results, experts are investigating the possibility of integrating blinatumomab early in the course of treating ALL. This challenges established paradigms and compels clinicians to reconsider the temporal dynamics of managing ALL patients by raising concerns about the best time to begin immunotherapy within the treatment trajectory. The precise timing of blinatumomab introduction necessitates a thorough assessment of the patient's response, the state of the disease, and the possibility of therapeutic synergies with other approaches.

Treatment recommendations also need to change to accommodate blinatumomab in clinical practice. Expert panels and regulatory bodies are in constant communication to update and improve guidelines to include blinatumomab as a standard therapeutic option for particular subsets of ALL patients, as evidence of its efficacy continues to mount. In order to guarantee that clinical guidelines appropriately and effectively reflect the changing landscape of ALL management, this process entails cooperative efforts between regulatory bodies, guideline committees, and experts.

The facilitation of the smooth integration of blinatumomab into clinical practice is largely dependent on educational initiatives. Physicians need up-to-date information and training on blinatumomab's distinct mechanisms of action, dosage concerns, possible side effects, and monitoring techniques. The provision of evidence-based resources, workshops, and educational programs are essential in enabling healthcare professionals to make well-informed decisions and offer the best possible care to patients with all types of illnesses.

In addition, the addition of blinatumomab presents issues with resource distribution, accessibility, and reimbursement. Crucial components of the implementation process include making sure that this novel therapy is available to qualified patients, resolving financial obstacles, and negotiating the complexities of reimbursement procedures. Optimizing patient access to blinatumomab and other transformative therapies requires cooperation between healthcare providers, payers, and pharmaceutical companies.

In conclusion, the medical community faces both a variety of opportunities and challenges when it comes to implementing blinatumomab into clinical practice. The successful integration of blinatumomab into routine ALL management is attributed to various factors, including the personalized approach to patient selection, treatment sequencing considerations, updates to guidelines, educational initiatives, and logistical and financial management. The goal of improving patient outcomes, raising the bar for care, and expanding the options for those dealing with the complications of acute lymphoblastic leukemia continue to be the main concerns of the medical community as it moves through this revolutionary stage.

Joint Research Projects and Continuing Studies

The release of trial results pertaining to the effectiveness of blinatumomab in treating Acute Lymphoblastic Leukemia (ALL) has sparked a wave of cooperative research projects and ongoing investigations among the scientific and medical communities. In response to the changing medical landscape, scientists, physicians, and pharmaceutical companies are actively involved in a variety of endeavors that are intended to deepen our understanding of the role of blinatumomab, reveal more aspects of its effectiveness, and investigate new combinations and applications in the context of hematological malignancies and ALL.

A prominent component of collaborative research projects is investigating the suitability of blinatumomab for use in particular subgroups of patients with ALL. In order to improve patient selection, ongoing research aims to identify the molecular and genetic profiles that might affect the response to blinatumomab. The goal is to find biomarkers or predictive factors that can help doctors customize blinatumomab treatment plans according to the particulars of each patient's illness. This precision medicine strategy, which emphasizes targeted interventions catered to the unique features of cancer biology, is consistent with the larger trend in oncology.

Additionally, blinatumomab's possible synergies with other immunotherapies and targeted agents are being investigated by researchers. In order to identify improved therapeutic effects and new treatment options for ALL, collaborative studies investigating combination therapies, such as the simultaneous use of blinatumomab and checkpoint inhibitors or small molecule inhibitors, are being conducted. These programs aim to maximize the complementary mechanisms of action for better patient outcomes while acknowledging the complex interactions between various modalities. Because these studies are collaborative in nature, academic institutions, pharmaceutical companies, and regulatory bodies work together to plan and carry out thorough investigations.

Key themes in ongoing research initiatives are the optimization of treatment sequencing and the investigation of early immunotherapy integration. Scholars are currently exploring whether blinatumomab's efficacy can be further increased by starting it earlier in the course of treatment or by combining it with other treatment modalities. These investigations encompass thorough evaluations of immunological responses, disease dynamics, and long-term results, offering valuable perspectives on the complex facets of blinatumomab's function in the changing context of ALL treatments. These studies are collaborative in nature and involve multidisciplinary teams, which promotes synergies between scientific inquiry and clinical expertise.

The trial results have prompted several questions, which are being investigated further. These include whether blinatumomab can be used in conjunction with other targeted therapies and whether it can be used in pediatric populations. The goal of collaborative efforts involving pediatric oncologists, pediatric hematological malignancy researchers, and industry partners is to provide children and adolescents with ALL with the advantages of blinatumomab. These programs highlight the dedication to diversity in research, acknowledging the special difficulties and possibilities related to the treatment of pediatric cancer.

Beyond the confines of individual studies, collaborative research initiatives form a network of interconnected efforts to advance our understanding of blinatumomab and its broader implications. The collaborative ecosystem that is fostered by the sharing of data, insights, and collective expertise speeds up scientific discovery and influences clinical practice. Frequent forums, conferences, and cooperative platforms serve as venues for knowledge exchange, guaranteeing that the combined efforts of the scientific and medical communities support the continuous advancement of ALL treatment approaches.

To sum up, joint research projects and continuing investigations highlight how blinatumomab is a dynamic and revolutionary drug in the context of ALL research. The spirit of cooperation between scientists, physicians, and business associates drives the search for new directions, opportunities for collaboration, and uses, influencing the course of treatment for hematological malignancies in the future. These joint efforts are a testament to the dedication to improving patient care, optimizing treatment strategies, and expanding the frontiers of scientific knowledge in the unwavering quest for better outcomes for those with acute lymphoblastic leukemia.

Conclusion

Blinatumomab's Importance in Developing Future Treatments for ALL

Thinking back on the path of treating Acute Lymphoblastic Leukemia (ALL) and the critical role that blinatumomab played, it is clear that this immunotherapeutic drug is a game-changer that will have a significant impact on how ALL is managed in the future. Beyond the confines of a single clinical trial, blinatumomab is significant because it is a beacon of hope that is changing treatment paradigms and pointing the way toward more patient-centered, focused, and effective approaches to ALL.

The significance of blinatumomab is found in its capacity to prolong survival as well as in its ability to refute accepted beliefs regarding the introduction and scheduling of immunotherapies in the course of treatment. The trial results have sparked debates regarding the integration of early immunotherapy, leading to a reassessment of the best times and methods to launch these novel treatments for optimal effectiveness. This change in viewpoint highlights how dynamically ALL research is conducted and calls on the medical community to continuously improve treatment plans in light of new research and patient-centered outcomes.

Blinatumomab has made a significant contribution in addressing the complexity of Minimal Residual Disease (MRD) and the implications of this condition for relapse. Blinatumomab has significantly changed our understanding of undetectable MRD by highlighting the importance of precisely targeting therapeutic interventions and proving the value of eliminating even the lowest levels of disease. Future decisions about risk assessment, treatment planning, and the creation of innovative therapeutic strategies that more aggressively address residual illness are guided by this realization.

Blinatumomab's unique mechanism of action as a bispecific T-cell engager (BiTE) contributes to its transformative role. Blanatumomab coordinates a focused immune response by simultaneously targeting T cells and cancer cells, demonstrating the efficacy of immunotherapies in managing the intricacies of hematological malignancies. The efficacy of blinatumomab in the treatment of ALL provides opportunities for investigating analogous tactics in other hematologic malignancies, promoting a more comprehensive comprehension of the suitability of biologic therapies and analogous immunotherapeutic methods.

The development of blinatumomab from clinical trials to possible incorporation into routine clinical practice is a prime example of the medical community's cooperative nature. Professionals, scientists, physicians, and pharmaceutical companies have collaborated to decipher the nuances of blinatumomab's effectiveness, experimenting with new combinations, improving treatment protocols, and attending to practical and budgetary issues. This cooperative synergy is a prime example of a shared dedication to improving patient care, expanding the field of scientific knowledge, and streamlining the ALL treatment environment.

Blinatumomab is a paradigm for precision medicine and a driving force behind ongoing research initiatives that will shape the future of ALL treatment. The field is dynamic and evolving due to the investigation of its role in particular patient subgroups, its potential combinations with targeted therapies, and its applicability in pediatric populations. The importance of blinatumomab in influencing ALL treatments going forward is not limited to its direct effects; it also encompasses the avenues it opens up for additional advancements, collaborations, and discoveries in the never-ending quest for better results for patients dealing with the intricacies of acute lymphoblastic leukemia.

At the nexus of scientific advancement and clinical application, blinatumomab represents a lighthouse of development, showing the path ahead in the search for more accurate, efficient, and patient-focused methods of treating ALL. The medical community's combined efforts, a dedication to groundbreaking research, and the unwavering hope for a day when ALL is defeated and each patient's path to remission is characterized by tenacity, creativity, and the promise of a better tomorrow all contribute to the ongoing journey.